DATE DUE

MR 18 '04			
MR 16 '10			
E 24 '10			

DEMCO 38-297

Cornerstones of Freedom

The Battle of Midway

TOM McGOWEN

CHILDREN'S PRESS®
A Division of Scholastic Inc.
New York • Toronto • London • Auckland • Sydney
Mexico City • New Delhi • Hong Kong
Danbury, Connecticut

Reading Consultant: Linda Cornwell, Coordinator of School Quality and
Professional Improvement, Indiana State Teachers Association

Content Consultant: Dr. Alan L. Gropman, Industrial College of the
Armed Forces

Visit Children's Press on the Internet at:
http://publishing.grolier.com

Library of Congress Cataloging-in-Publication Data

McGowen, Tom.
   The Battle of Midway / Tom McGowen.
      p. cm.— (Cornerstones of freedom)
Includes index.
   ISBN 0-516-22005-5 (lib-bdg.)   0-516-25956-3 (pbk.)
   1. Midway, Battle of, 1942—Juvenile literature. [1. Midway, Battle of,
1942. 2. World War, 1939–1945—Naval operations.] I. Title. II. Series.
D774.M5 M347   2001
940.54'26—dc221
                                        00-030330

As the year 1941 ended, Americans were grim and worried. Only three weeks before—on December 7, 1941—the Empire of Japan launched a surprise bombing attack on the U.S. naval base at Pearl Harbor, Hawaii. The attack was disastrous for the U.S. Pacific Fleet. Two battleships sank, one turned over, and five others were severely damaged. The Japanese destroyed more than 260 American airplanes, killed some two thousand men, and injured more than a thousand more. The United States declared war on Japan, entering World War II (1941–1945).

The battleships USS West Virginia *(foreground) and USS* Tennessee *(background) burn following the Japanese attack on Pearl Harbor on December 7, 1941.*

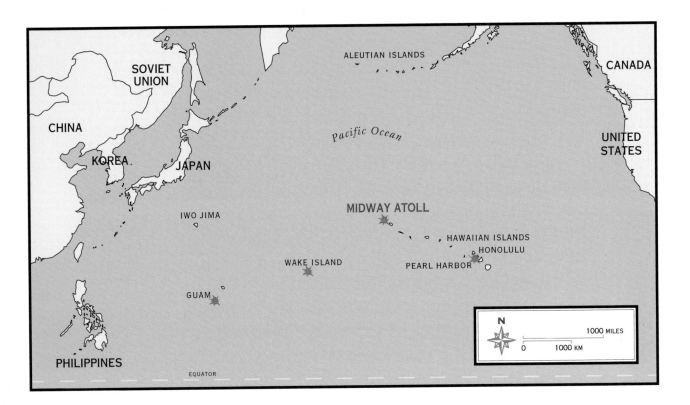

Within the map:

SOVIET UNION

ALEUTIAN ISLANDS

CANADA

CHINA

Pacific Ocean

UNITED STATES

KOREA

JAPAN

IWO JIMA

MIDWAY ATOLL

HAWAIIAN ISLANDS

HONOLULU

WAKE ISLAND

PEARL HARBOR

GUAM

N

1000 MILES

0   1000 KM

PHILIPPINES

EQUATOR

Can you guess how Midway got its name? Look at the atoll's position between North America and Asia.

Within days of the Pearl Harbor bombing, Japanese forces attacked two other important U.S. naval bases in the Pacific Ocean—the Philippine Islands and the island of Guam. Two weeks later, the Japanese captured the U.S. naval base at Wake Island. The Americans were losing.

To make matters worse, Germany and Italy had also declared war on the United States. German submarines sank American ships in the Atlantic Ocean. Although the United States had constructed a two-ocean navy, U.S. forces would be tested in both the Atlantic and Pacific during this terrible, worldwide war.

During the first three months of 1942, the bad situation got even worse. The United Kingdom and the Netherlands, two countries on the same side as the United States, were being defeated. Japanese forces invaded the Dutch East Indies (now known as Indonesia), and they captured an army of 70,000 British soldiers in Singapore. The American forces in the Philippines were steadily losing ground to the Japanese. The Empire of Japan was like an invincible whirlwind. Many Americans feared that Japanese troops would soon invade the West Coast of the United States.

Then something happened that encouraged people throughout the United States. On April 18, 1942, sixteen U.S. Army Air Force B-25 bombers bombed four Japanese cities. Americans believed that they had finally struck a blow against the enemy. The attack did not really do much damage, but it lifted the spirits of the American people.

On the other hand, the bombing shocked and enraged the Japanese. Japan's leaders were puzzled and worried. Such an air attack seemed impossible. A B-25 bomber could fly about 1,350 miles (2,173 kilometers) with a full tank of gas. The nearest U.S. naval base to Japan, known as Midway, was more than 2,000 miles (3,200 km) away. Where had the planes come from?

The bombers had taken off from an aircraft carrier, the USS *Hornet*. This ship was in the Pacific Ocean about 650 miles (1,040 km) from Japan. Most experts did not think a B-25 could take off from a ship because the big, heavy plane was designed to take off only from land. However, the crews of the sixteen bombers had trained until they could take off from an aircraft carrier deck successfully.

This possibility did not occur to Japanese military leaders. They thought that the bombers must have flown from Midway, perhaps using extra or special fuel tanks. They wanted to capture Midway so that the Americans could not launch more air attacks from the base against the Japanese.

Midway was one of the U.S. Navy's best bases in the Pacific Ocean. Midway is an atoll, or a ring-shaped coral island surrounding a small area of ocean water. Midway Atoll is two islands and an area of watery sand inside an incomplete coral ring. This ring forms a perfect harbor for a number of ships, and the two islands are large enough for airfields.

Sixteen U.S. Army B-25 bombers took off from the deck of the USS Hornet *to attack Japan in April 1942.*

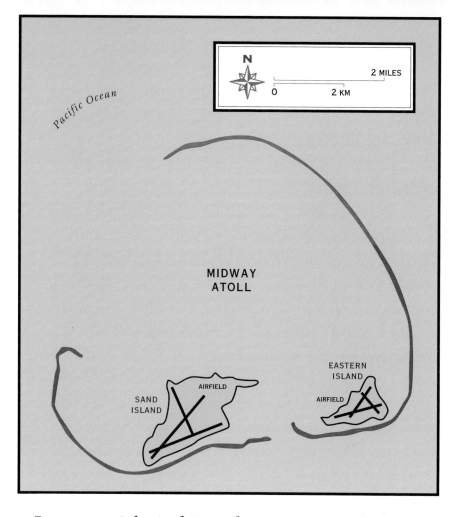

2 MILES

0   2 KM

Pacific Ocean

MIDWAY
ATOLL

EASTERN
ISLAND

AIRFIELD

AIRFIELD

SAND
ISLAND

*The coral reef
surrounding Sand
Island and Eastern
Island creates the
protected harbor
of Midway Atoll.*

Japanese Admiral Isoroku Yamamoto believed
that if Japan captured Midway, the U.S. Pacific
Fleet would attempt to take it back. He intended
to trap the Americans by attacking Midway.
Yamamoto was in command of the Japanese
fleet, and he had planned the bombing of Pearl
Harbor. Even though that attack was successful,
he did not think it had done enough damage. No
American aircraft carriers had been hit then, so
the U.S. fleet was still powerful. Yamamoto
believed that unless Japan quickly destroyed
the U.S. fleet, Japan would lose the war.

Admiral Yamamoto had lived in the United States as a member of the Japanese embassy staff. He had studied American ways. He knew that if the war stretched out for more than a year, the United States could win because American industry could produce more warships than Japanese industry. However, he thought if Japan could destroy most of the U.S. Pacific Fleet, Americans would think there was no hope of beating Japan. Then, the United States might settle for peace.

Admiral Yamamoto's battle plan for destroying the U.S. Pacific Fleet and capturing Midway was complicated. He planned to form his force into five widely separated groups of ships. One group would attack the American bases in the Aleutian Islands, off the coast of Alaska. Yamamoto hoped this attack would lure some ships away from the U.S. Pacific Fleet to defend the Aleutian bases. Yamamoto's other four groups would wait to come together quickly and surround the remaining U.S. Pacific Fleet. First, a group containing four aircraft carriers would launch planes to bomb the American ships. Then groups of battleships and cruisers would move in with their big guns to finish off the Americans.

Some Japanese leaders had disagreed with Yamamoto's plan. But when the B-25s bombed Japanese cities, they began to think he might be

Fleet Admiral Isoroku Yamamoto, commander of the Japanese Fleet, planned the attacks on Pearl Harbor and Midway.

right. Then something happened that brought them into full agreement with him. A Japanese fleet went to capture the important base of Port Moresby, on the island of Papua New Guinea, near Australia. On May 7, 1942, the Japanese fleet ran into a force of American ships in a stretch of water known as the Coral Sea.

A battle took place, now called the Battle of the Coral Sea. The Americans lost the big aircraft carrier *Lexington*, a destroyer, and a tanker. The Japanese lost a small aircraft carrier and several other ships. The battle was technically a draw, but the Japanese had to turn back and give up the invasion. Japanese leaders decided that Yamamoto was right—the Japanese Navy needed to capture Midway and destroy the remainder of the U.S. Pacific Fleet.

The crew of the Lexington *abandons ship as the aircraft carrier begins to sink during the Battle of the Coral Sea.*

Soon after the Battle of the Coral Sea, Admiral Yamamoto began building up a force to capture Midway. By May 26, 1942, it was ready. The force contained four of Japan's biggest aircraft carriers. Together, these ships carried 272 planes. Two small carriers transported thirty-one additional planes. Along with the aircraft carriers, there were eleven battleships, sixteen cruisers, and forty-five destroyers. There were also fifteen submarines. Many ships carried troops and supplies for the invasion of Midway. The Japanese force sailed on May 27, 1942. Each of the five groups took a different route.

The Japanese fleet was much larger than the U.S. Pacific Fleet, especially in numbers of aircraft carriers and battleships. Admiral Yamamoto and the other Japanese leaders were completely confident of victory. They were also sure that they would catch the Americans by surprise.

As the Japanese force was being put together, however, officers at the Japanese naval headquarters sent coded radio messages to many Japanese ships. Radios on American ships and at U.S. naval bases picked up those messages, and they were quickly decoded. The U.S. Navy had figured out the Japanese Navy's secret code! From the decoded messages, Admiral Chester W. Nimitz, commander-in-chief of the U.S. Pacific Fleet, knew the Japanese military leaders' plans. He had a good idea of the size and makeup of Admiral

Admiral Chester W. Nimitz was appointed commander of the U.S. Pacific Fleet after the attack on Pearl Harbor.

Yamamoto's force. Admiral Nimitz was also almost certain when the attack would happen. The attack on Midway was *not* going to be a surprise.

Admiral Nimitz called every available American warship to Pearl Harbor to form a fleet to defend Midway. The fleet was made up of two groups of ships that were known as Task Forces 16 and 17. Task Force 16 consisted of the aircraft carriers *Hornet* and *Enterprise*, six cruisers, and nine destroyers. Task Force 17 was made up of the aircraft carrier *Yorktown*, two cruisers, and six destroyers. There was also a group of twelve submarines. Against the Japanese force of ninety-three fighting ships, the Americans had only thirty-eight.

Rear Admiral Frank Jack Fletcher had commanded the American force in the Coral Sea. Now, he was in charge of the operation to defend Midway and the commander of Task Force 17.

Rear Admiral Frank Jack Fletcher commanded the U.S. battle fleets at the Battle of the Coral Sea and the Battle of Midway.

Rear Admiral Raymond A. Spruance— a calm man and a careful, logical thinker—commanded Task Force 16. While the two navy task forces were forming, the U.S. Navy sent more marines, guns, and planes to defend Midway. The defenders planted explosive mines in the water around the atoll, strung barbed wire around the beaches, and dug bombproof shelters deep into the coral. Midway became a fortress.

Task Force 16 left Pearl Harbor on May 28, 1942. Task Force 17's aircraft carrier, *Yorktown*, had been severely damaged in the Battle of the Coral Sea. People worked day and night to repair the ship. Miraculously, Task Force 17 sailed on May 30. Three days later, the two forces came together at a point in the Pacific Ocean 325 miles (520 km) from Midway. There, they sat and waited. The submarines glided silently through the waters around Midway, watching for enemy ships. Patrols of Navy PBY flying boats, known as "Catalinas," flew over the ocean to a distance of 700 miles (1127 km) in all directions from Midway. These patrols were also watching for the approaching Japanese fleet.

U.S. Navy PBY flying boats, called Catalinas, flew patrols over the ocean around Midway. Crew members searched for the approaching Japanese forces.

This PBY Catalina crew first sighted a Japanese fleet near Midway: (back row, from left to right) R.J. Derouin, Francis Musser, Co-pilot Hardeman, Pilot J.H. Reid, and R.A. Swan; (front row, left to right) J.F. Gammell, J. Goovers, and P.A. Fitzpatrick.

At 9:20 A.M. on the morning of June 3, 1942, a Catalina was flying southwest of Midway. The pilot spotted eleven Japanese ships sailing toward Midway. He sent a message reporting that the Japanese fleet was on its way.

Admiral Fletcher had a decision to make. Should he move his forces toward the enemy ships that had been sighted? He did not believe that the main Japanese force would come from the southwest. So he ordered his forces to sail northwest.

Admiral Fletcher made the right decision. The ships that the Catalina pilot had seen were merely troop ships carrying Japanese soldiers to Midway. By sailing northwest, the American ships were heading straight for the main Japanese aircraft carrier force.

Unaware that American ships were in the area, Japanese commanders prepared for their attack on Midway. Vice Admiral Chuichi Nagumo commanded the fleet containing the four big aircraft carriers. At 4:30 A.M. on June 4, 1942, Nagumo ordered his aircraft carriers to launch 108 planes.

The Japanese force that was about to attack Midway was made up of three groups of planes. About a third of them were dive bombers. They carried one heavy bomb or two light ones. Dive bombers attacked by swooping almost straight down at a target and dropping a bomb. Another third of the Japanese planes were torpedo bombers. Torpedo bombers flew straight at an enemy ship and dropped a single torpedo. For the attack on Midway, they were armed with bombs to drop on buildings and airfields. The remaining third of the planes were fast, well-armed fighter planes called Zeros. The Zeros job was to attack and shoot down any enemy fighter planes that tried to attack the bombers.

Vice Admiral Chuichi Nagumo commanded the four main aircraft carriers of the Japanese fleet attacking Midway.

About an hour after the Japanese planes took off, an American Catalina flying on patrol from Midway spotted them heading for Midway. The pilot immediately radioed a message to Midway and every American ship.

So, Admiral Fletcher knew the location of the enemy ships. He ordered Admiral Spruance to take Task Force 16 toward the Japanese fleet and launch an air attack from the *Hornet* and *Enterprise*. Fletcher would bring Task Force 17 to join Spruance.

These Japanese Zero fighter planes are being prepared for takeoff on the deck of an aircraft carrier.

On Midway, sirens were howling and planes were taking off. Most of the American fighter planes were older and slower than the Zeros. Of twenty-seven American planes that went up to defend Midway, seventeen were shot down. Seven others were badly damaged. The Japanese lost only five planes.

With nothing to stop the Japanese bombers and torpedo planes, they came roaring over the atoll. Some of the Japanese planes were shot down by anti-aircraft fire, but the rest dropped their bombs. As they were leaving, however, the Japanese commander saw that the air strike had not really been successful. Midway's airfields and defenses were still in good shape. The commander radioed a message to Admiral Nagumo that said, "There is need for a second attack wave."

However, Admiral Nagumo's fleet was under attack by groups of U.S. Navy torpedo planes, Marine dive bombers, and Army Air Force bombers. These planes took off from Midway before the Japanese planes arrived. The Zeros patrolling overhead attacked the American aircraft. The destroyers and cruisers guarding the four Japanese aircraft carriers opened fire with their anti-aircraft guns. The American planes were simply shot out of the sky or driven off—many badly damaged. No Japanese ship was damaged during this attack.

This U.S. plane was damaged during the attack on Midway

At 7:15 A.M., Admiral Nagumo ordered his aircraft carriers to prepare another air strike on Midway. Thirteen minutes later, a Japanese scout plane reported sighting American ships. Nagumo had not expected to face enemy ships. Now, he had to make a serious decision. He decided to cancel the attack on Midway and launch an attack on the enemy ships instead.

Preparation for an attack on the ships took time, however, because the torpedo planes had been armed with bombs to drop on Midway. Now the Japanese had to rearm their planes with torpedoes to launch at the enemy ships. As the rearming began, Nagumo ordered his fleet to change course and head north—where the American ships were.

At just about this same time, Admiral Spruance, Task Force 16's commander, also made an important decision. His aircraft carriers were now close enough to the Japanese fleet that American planes could attack. Spruance had to decide whether to attack the Japanese immediately or hold his planes in readiness to defend against a Japanese attack. He decided to take a risk and try to strike the first blow with an all-out attack. At 7:52 A.M., Task Force 16 began launching 116 planes against the Japanese.

A flight of thirty-seven dive bombers and nine fighters from the *Hornet* was the first to reach the point where Admiral Nagumo's fleet was supposed to be. The Japanese fleet was no longer there. The flight commander had to

Douglas Dauntless dive bombers from the Hornet *attack a Japanese aircraft carrier on June 6, 1942.*

decide quickly where to find the enemy. He signaled a turn to the south—the wrong way—but a squadron of fifteen torpedo bombers from the *Hornet* headed north. So did a squadron of torpedo bombers and two dive bomber squadrons from the *Enterprise*. By this time, Task Force 17 and the *Yorktown* were within range of the Japanese. Task Force 17 launched torpedo planes and dive bombers. They, too, headed the right way.

Hornet's fifteen torpedo bombers reached Admiral Nagumo's ships first. Flying low over the water, the bombers headed for the aircraft carriers. From high overhead, Zeros dove on the torpedo bombers. The American planes were simply no match for the Zeros. Every bomber was shot down. Not a single torpedo struck a Japanese ship.

Torpedo bombers get ready for takeoff from the deck of the U.S. aircraft carrier Enterprise.

The *Yorktown* squadron attacked the third Japanese aircraft carrier, *Soryu*. One of the squadron's bombs exploded on the hangar deck. Two others demolished the flight deck. *Soryu* was ablaze. In only five or six minutes, Japan lost three of its aircraft carriers. The Battle of Midway had turned in favor of the United States!

The last Japanese aircraft carrier, *Hiryu*, had become separated from the rest of Admiral Nagumo's fleet. No American dive bombers had seen *Hiryu*. There were eighteen dive bombers and six Zeros on its flight deck, and more planes on the hangar deck below, ready to go. *Hiryu*'s commander, Rear Admiral Yamaguchi, knew that his planes should follow the American planes. They would lead the Japanese planes straight to the American aircraft carriers. Yamaguchi ordered his planes launched.

The planes that the Japanese pilots chose to follow were from the *Yorktown*. The Japanese sighted the *Yorktown* at just about noon and immediately attacked. Twelve Wildcat fighter planes defending the *Yorktown* attempted to stop the Japanese planes before they could get to the aircraft carrier. The Wildcats shot down ten Japanese dive bombers, but eight escaped fire. The cruisers and destroyers around *Yorktown* opened fire with their anti-aircraft guns but scored no hits. Three bombs struck the *Yorktown*. The explosions caused several fires, carved a hole in the flight deck, and knocked out the aircraft carrier's communications system.

The *Yorktown* was Admiral Fletcher's flagship. With its communications system gone, he could not contact any other ships. He left the aircraft carrier and went aboard a nearby cruiser. He sent word to Admiral Spruance to command the rest of the battle. The *Yorktown* was not badly hurt. Soon the fires were put out and the flight deck was repaired. By 2:00 P.M., the *Yorktown* was ready to fight again.

Smokes rolls from the U.S. aircraft carrier Yorktown *after three Japanese bombs hit the ship.*

Then ten torpedo planes and six Zero fighters from *Hiryu* appeared. American fighter planes rushed at the torpedo bombers and Zeros, and the ships opened fire with anti-aircraft guns again. Four torpedo planes escaped fire. Two torpedoes exploded against the *Yorktown's* hull— blowing a hole in it, knocking out the ship's electrical power, and jamming the rudder so the ship could not steer. With water pouring into the *Yorktown* through the hole, the aircraft carrier began to lean to one side. The crew was ordered to leave the sinking ship. *Hiryu's* planes had done their job.

The Yorktown *is under attack during the Battle of Midway. The black smudges in the sky are smoke from bursting shells of anti-aircraft guns.*

American scouting planes from the *Enterprise* located the *Hiryu* at 2:45 P.M. By 4:00 P.M., forty dive bombers from the *Enterprise* and *Hornet* were flying toward the Japanese aircraft carrier. One hour later, sixteen bombers from the *Enterprise* arrived and immediately attacked the *Hiryu*. No one saw them coming. When the Japanese sailors heard the sound of the shrill, ever-increasing scream of the dive bombers' engines, they were shocked. The first bomb blew a hole in the *Hiryu*'s flight deck. More bombs started fires that spread quickly. Soon, the *Hiryu* was blazing furiously and drifting out of control.

This aerial photograph of the Hiryu *shows the Japanese aircraft carrier burning and sinking after being hit by American dive bombers.*

Admiral Yamamoto was hundreds of miles away with the main fleet. When he learned that the Americans destroyed all four of his main aircraft carriers, he was stunned and horrified. However, he still had eleven battleships and sixteen cruisers. With their big guns, those ships could blow the American aircraft carriers out of the water and turn certain defeat into victory. Yamamoto ordered his remaining ships to attack the U.S. fleet.

Admiral Spruance expected that Admiral Yamamoto might try such an attack, and Spruance had no intention of getting caught

Rear Admiral Raymond A. Spruance ordered the air strikes that won the Battle of Midway.

in a gun battle his force could not win. He ordered Task Force 16 to pull back well out of reach. The Japanese ships searched for the American ships through the night, but they did not find them. At 2:55 A.M on the morning of June 5, Yamamoto ordered his fleet to return, and he sent a brief message to every Japanese ship. The message said, "Occupation of Midway cancelled." The attempt to capture Midway and destroy the U.S. Pacific Fleet had failed.

Yamamoto's officers wondered how they could notify the emperor of such a terrible defeat.

"I am the only one who must apologize to His Majesty," Yamamoto told them. The Battle of Midway was not quite over, though. During the next two days, American planes located two Japanese cruisers and sank one with bombs. A Japanese submarine fired two torpedoes into the *Yorktown* while it was still afloat and being towed to Pearl Harbor. The *Yorktown* sank early the next morning, on June 7, 1942.

The sinking of the *Yorktown* finally ended the Battle of Midway. Japan lost four aircraft carriers, one cruiser, 275 airplanes, and 3,500 Japanese. The United States lost one carrier, one destroyer, 132 airplanes, and 307 Americans. The United States still controlled Midway.

Marines on Midway stand before the flag-draped bodies of their comrades who were killed during the Japanese air attack.

Navy pilot Ensign George Gay was shot down during the Battle of Midway. He was later rescued and taken to a naval hospital in Honolulu, Hawaii. In this photograph, he and a nurse share the news of the victory at Midway.

When Americans heard the news of the victory at Midway, they cheered and celebrated. Americans believed that the war had turned— and it had. Midway was what military historians call a decisive battle—one that wins a war or leads to the winning of a war. Some years after the war, Admiral Nimitz said, "Midway was the most crucial battle of the Pacific War, the engagement that made everything else possible."

The loss of four aircraft carriers, many aircraft, and experienced naval pilots, crippled the Japanese Navy. With American shipbuilders rapidly producing new aircraft carriers and other kinds of ships, the strength of the U.S. Navy grew—just as Yamamoto had feared. After Midway, the United States went on the offensive until Japan surrendered on September 2, 1945. World War II was finally over.

A cheering crowd in New York City's Times Square celebrates the Japanese surrender.

GLOSSARY

The aircraft carrier
Lexington

aircraft carrier – a large naval ship designed as an air base at sea from which aircraft can takeoff and land

atoll – a ring-shaped coral island or string of islands consisting of a reef and surrounding a small area of ocean water

B-25 bomber – a propeller-driven bombing plane with two engines, one on each wing

base – an island or coastal harbor that is a protected center for military or naval operations

battleship – heavily armored vessels with huge, powerful guns

cruiser – a vessel that is smaller than a battleship, but faster, and heavily armored and armed

destroyer – small, fast, lightly armored ships that protect aircraft carriers from submarines

flagship – the ship carrying the commander of a group of ships

fleet – a group of warships under one command

harbor – a part of a body of water so protected that it is a safe place for ships to drop anchor

hull – the frame or body of a ship

offensive – an attack in warfare

rudder – a movable flat piece attached at the rear of a ship or aircraft for steering

squadron – a group of military airplanes or naval ships moving and working together

superstructure – the part of a ship above the main deck containing various compartments for commanding and controlling the ship

torpedo – a bomb-shaped, explosive missile that moves through water toward an enemy ship

torpedo bomber – a single-engine airplane that carried a torpedo or bomb

Torpedo bombers on the deck of the Enterprise

TIMELINE

1941  *December 7:* The Japanese attack Pearl Harbor

June 3: 9:20 A.M. U.S. Navy pilot spots Japanese ships heading for Midway

1942

June 4: 4:30 A.M. Japanese aircraft carriers launch planes to attack Midway

5:30 A.M. American scout plane spots Japanese aircraft carriers

June 5: 2:55 A.M. Admiral Yamamoto cancels the invasion of Midway

6:20 A.M. Admiral Fletcher orders Admiral Spruance's Task Force 16 to head toward Japanese aircraft carriers

June 6: 1:30 P.M. A Japanese submarine torpedoes the *Yorktown*

6:30 A.M. Planes from Admiral Nagumo's aircraft carriers begin air attack

June 7: 6:00 A.M. The *Yorktown* sinks

7:10 A.M. American planes from Midway attack Nagumo's fleet with no result

7:52 A.M. Admiral Spruance orders airstrike on Nagumo's fleet

9:25 A.M. U.S. fleet torpedo bomber squadrons begin attack on Nagumo's fleet

10:26 A.M. U.S. dive bomber squadrons disable three Japanese aircraft carriers

12:00 NOON *Hiryu's* dive bombers attack and damage *Yorktown*

2:45 P.M. U.S. scout planes locate *Hiryu*

5:00 P.M. Dive bombers from *Enterprise* attack and disable *Hiryu*

1945 *September 2:* The Japanese surrender

INDEX (**Boldface** page numbers indicate illustrations)

PHOTO CREDITS

Photographs ©: AP/Wide World Photos: 10, 19, 30 bottom; Corbis-Bettmann: 3, 26, 29, 31 top right, 31 bottom, (UPI), 6, 8, 9, 11, 13, 14, 15, 17, 24, 27, 28, 30 top; Liaison Agency, Inc.: 12 (Hulton Getty); Naval Historical Foundation: 25 (Courtesy of Mr. Kazutoshi Hando, Tokyo), cover, 2, 18, 21, 23, 31 top left; U.S. Naval Academy Photo: 1. Maps by: TJS Design

PICTURE IDENTIFICATIONS

Cover: An artist depicts American planes attacking a Japanese cruiser during the Battle of Midway.
Page 1: The Midway Memorial is at the U.S. Naval Academy in Annapolis, Maryland.
Page 2: This aerial photograph of Midway Atoll was taken in November 1941. Eastern Island is in the foreground and Sand Island is in the background.

ABOUT THE AUTHOR

Tom McGowen is a children's author with a special interest in military history. His most recent book in the Cornerstones of Freedom series was *The Battle for Iwo Jima*. A fifteen-year old at the time of the Battle of Midway, McGowen later served in the U.S. Navy during the final year of World War II. He has authored fifty-four books for young readers—fiction and nonfiction. He was the 1990 winner of the Children's Reading Round Table Annual Award for Outstanding Contributions to the Field of Children's Literature and is in *Who's Who in America*.